Look At My God! 6

(Victories in Evangelism)

Pastor Paul M. Caprietta

Look at My God! 6
Victories in Evangelism
Las Vegas
Pastor Paul M. Caprietta
Copyright © 2022

ISBN: 9798352164648

Published by Pastor Paul M. Caprietta
Pico Rivera, CA

Printed in the United States of America

Foundational Scripture

"I thank my Christ Jesus our Lord, who has given me strength; that he considered me trustworthy, appointing me to his service. Even though I was once a blasphemer and a prosecutor and a violent man. I was shown mercy because I acted in ignorance and unbelief. The grace of our Lord was poured out on me abundantly, along with the faith and love that are in Christ Jesus."

1 Timothy 1:12-14

"I have heard the vice of the Lord saying, "whom shall I send? And who will go for us?" And I said, "Here am I, send me."

Isaiah 6:8

"However, I consider my life worth nothing to me; my only aim is to finish the race and complete the task the Lord Jesus has given me – the task of testifying to the good news of God's grace."

Acts 20:24

Preface

I wrote this book to document twelve of my evangelistic experiences I have had over my many years of sharing the gospel of Jesus Christ on a one-on-one basis for the past twenty-nine years of ministry/ I have decided to document these encounters which I believe will challenge and inspire you to share the gospel, which is in my opinion the greatest news available with the people you meet daily. I met so many people through my daily activities, and I am moved with compassion to minister to the needs of people who are hurting and in need of a savior.

I am a licensed and ordained Pastor for many years and in ministry for over twenty-nine. I have a desire to see people saved and come into the knowledge of the truth. I am very perplexed when some Christians do not share their faith in Jesus Christ with others for several reasons of which I will try to give you some of my rational as to why some people refuse to share the gospel with others.

Therefore, what I have seen is that some Christians feel that they need to know the entire Bible or most of the Bible. Secondly, others are due to fear of being rejected or they are just timid. Thirdly, others said that sharing the gospel is for the five-fold ministry, which God have equipped to do. Unfortunately, this last reason is further from the truth.

My desire is that this book will jumpstart your faith in reaching out to the world who so desperately need an intimate relationship Jesus Christ as their personal savior and Lord of their lives. I am reminded by the teachings found in the Holy Bible.

The word of God teaches,

Jesus said to them, "Go into all the world and preach the gospel to al creation."

Mark 16:15

The word of God said, go and the word go is an action word which means to do something to achieve a result. The question I am asking you my reader, are you being obedient by following the instructions of our savior? We must do our part in being obedient to God and allow God's Holy Spirit to work through us. Trust me, you will get the results if you are willing and obedient to your master, in the personality of Jesus Christ, whom is the person who commissioned you to do his work on the earth. I am a living testimony of being obedient to share the gospel of Jesus Christ and bring men, women, and children to Jesus Christ.

Who should read this book?

Anyone wanting to minister to the needs of people and have a compassion to lead people to Jesus Christ. There are so many people in need of our savior's help and unfortunately some Christians are just playing church and are not trying to aid in meeting the spiritual needs of others.

As Christians, we should be looking for ways to reach out to others so they can come into a true and dynamic relationship with Jesus Christ. People are hurting and in need of a savior. We are called to share the gospel of Jesus Christ with as many people as possible and led by the Holy Spirit convict them of their sins. We should concentrate on what matters to God and what matters to God should matter to us as well, which is soul winning and more soul winning for the kingdom of God.

If you are truly willing to lead people to Jesus Christ, take time to pray and seek the Lord and be moved with the spirit of compassion. I do not have any formula for leading people to Jesus Christ, but I am moved by the spirit of Jesus Christ, and I say what the spirit of God directs me to say. May the spirit of God fall upon you, my reader and may you lead people to Jesus Christ like never before in your life. Stay committed to bringing people into the kingdom of God for his glory and honor. Remember, depend on the spirit of God for direction.

May you be inspired to win the lost at any cost. We can do it individually and collectively in Jesus' name.

The Bible teaches,

"He said to them, "Go into all the world and preach the gospel to all creation."

Mark 16:15

Contents

Chapter 12

Introduction

Introduction
How it started

I received a phone call on one sunny Saturday afternoon in July 2016 from a young lady. The name and number showed up on my caller ID as Gail. I took the call, and the person said is this "Rev. Paul Caprietta," I responded by saying yes and whom I am speaking too. She said, "my name is Gail, and I was you co-worker at a school in Trinidad from 1985 thru 1989 and do you remember me." I said yes, I do.

She said, "I was browsing the internet for you and your name came up as Rev. Paul Caprietta and she said, I was surprised that you are a Pastor now and I remembered you telling us in the school office in 1988 that you will become a Pastor one day preaching the word of God and we all laughed at you for making such a statement."

When my wife, Gail, came home from work I shared with her the conversation I just had with a past co-worker of mine many years ago in Trinidad and she was utterly amazed by what I said. I told Gail, my wife, I recalled making that statement in the summer of 1988 while working at that school in Trinidad as a Computer Science Lecturer. Some of the staff members were sitting in the school office talking about many topics about school, family, and life. When suddenly I said to my co-workers that I will be a Pastor preaching the word of God one day.

I did not know why I made that statement, but it was the call of God upon my life that allow that statement to come out of my mouth. I was not even a Christian at that time, but God knew that I was one of his chosen servants to proclaim the gospel of Jesus Christ to a lost and dying world. A year later in 1989 I left the institution for another one and while working at the new institution I accepted Jesus Christ as my personal savior and Lord all to the glory of God.

On the morning of September 18, 2016, my wife and I was talking about the goodness of God in and upon my life when I called Gail my past co-worker who now live in Brooklyn, New York and she shared the same information with my wife I made in 1988. God is truly an impressive God.

The Bible declares,

"Before I formed you in the womb I knew you, before you were born, I set you apart; I appointed you as a prophet to the nations."

Jeremiah 1:5

To my surprise I received a call from Gail, my former co-worker on Saturday 29 July 2017, we spoke about life in Trinidad and how things are going on with each of us. When suddenly I felt an unction from the Holy Spirit to share the gospel of Jesus Christ with her. The word of God went forth with clarity, power and purpose and she later said, "yes to Jesus Christ as her personal savior and Lord." She was so excited to accept Jesus Christ as her personal savior and Lord. She further reminded me that I can call her anytime so we can pray.

I was overwhelmed by her remarks of saying I can call her and pray with her anytime. God is truly an impressive, loving, and compassionate God to whomever decide to accept Him as their personal savior and Lord. Gail my fellow co-worker and my wife Gail were partially responsible for me drafting this book for people to be motivated and to fulfil the call of God upon their lives and win the lost for Jesus Christ – our soon and coming King. My other co-workers gave their lives to Jesus Christ as well. The last member of the staff called me on Sunday April 4, 2022, over the phone because he got my number from a former staff member, and I shared the great news of Jesus Christ with him, and he prayed the salvation prayer to receive Jesus Christ as his personal savior and Lord. Thank you, Jesus, for using me to bring three of my four former co-workers to you. LOOK at my God.

The Bible teaches,

The fruit of the righteous is a tree of life, and the one who is wise saves lives."

Proverbs 11:30

Chapter 1

The twelve workings

Chapter 1

The twelve workings

I have decided to document twelve experiences because the number twelve is especially important in the Bible and important to me. The number twelve stands for a perfect number. It symbolizes God's power and authority. When Jesus Christ went to hell, he took the keys of death and the grave and he gave the power and authority to the church, which is the body of Christ. The Bible teaches,

"I will give you the keys of the kingdom of heaven; whatever you bind on earth shall be bound in heaven, and whatever you lose on earth will be loose in heaven."

Matthew 16:19

"The sting of death is sin, and the power of sin is the law."

1 Corinthians 15:56

The number twelve is the number of perfections. That was the reason Jesus Chose twelve disciples because he chose twelve to change the world, and we are his disciple's bringing salvation to the world for those who accept Him as their personal savior and Lord.

The word salvation in the Greek language is "SOZO" which means completely whole. Jesus Christ gave us the power and authority so that we can help make us, his people completely whole in Him. We serve a perfect and glorious God.

The Bible teaches,

"The Lord will vindicate: your love, Lord, endures forever-do not abandon the works of your hands."

Psalm 138:8

We are his disciples because we are his followers, students, and joint heirs with Him bringing hope and deliverance to a loss and dying world. We are His disciples, and we must follow the commands and statues of God bringing light to a dark and callous world. I am one of His disciples who are working to conduct the assignment God has called you and me to do which is to bring people into a closer relationship with Jesus Christ.

Throughout this book, you will notice the love and compassion I have shown to the people I brought into a closer relationship with Jesus Christ. It takes a lot of effort and lots of compassion to steer people to Jesus Christ. Remember, God is a God of compassion, and He wishes none perish but all come into a knowledge of the truth, there are several significances of the number twelve.

Listed below are a few illustrations of the power use of the number twelve: -

- Jesus started his earthly ministry at twelve years old in the temple.
- Jesus had twelve disciples.
- There are twelve apostles.
- There are twelve tribes of Israel.
- There are twelve legions of Angels.
- Jesus sitting upon twelve thrones.
- Judging the twelve tribes of Israel
- In Orthodox Judaism twelve signifies the age a girl matures
- There are twelve great feasts.
- In Hinduism, the sun god Surya has twelve names.
- There are twelve calendar months.
- There are twelve months in a year.
- There are twelve jurors.
- There is a twelve-step program to recovery.
- In the Book of Revelation there was a wall great and high and had twelve gates.
- The gates twelve angels

Based on the information listed above you can appreciate the importance of the number twelve both spiritually and in society. Hence the reason I have decided to illustrate twelve scenarios of my evangelistic outreaches for my reader to glean by and to complete the work God had commissioned all his disciples to do on the earth. God is calling everyone of us in the body of Christ to do the work of an evangelist.

The Scripture teaches,

"But you, keep your head in all situations, endure hardship, do the work of an evangelist, discharge all the duties of your ministry."

2 Timothy 4:5

Why were we in Las Vegas?

My wonderful and adorable children came together and decided to send us on a trip for our 25-wedding anniversary. We had visited Las Vegas several years ago, so given the opportunity to visit there again was a tremendous prospect for us. We packed our bags together with five Bibles, rented a car, and travelled to Las Vegas to enjoy a week of celebration to enjoy a wonderful time together. The reason I decided to pack five Bibles is since I have an evangelistic mindset. Anywhere the Lord take me is an opportunity to share the gospel of Jesus Christ.

A lot of people have a strange concept of Las Vegas as being a sin City. I choose to see it differently, because wherever the Lord direct my steps as mentioned previously, I see it as an opportunity to minister the gospel of Jesus Christ with as many people and steer them into a relationship with Jesus Christ as their personal savior and Lord, all for the glory of my heavenly father.

The Bible teaches,

"The law was brought in so that the trespass might increase. But where sin increased, grace increased even more."

Romans 5:20

I hate to label any place, as a place where God cannot reach. People look at Las Vegas as a sin city. However, I took at Las Vegas as salvation city as mentioned above and see a greater opportunity for God's Holy Spirit to be manifested and his glory to be seen on the earth. Las Vegas can be a place where a great move of God can be manifested if people with the right concept of God choose to help liberate the place instead of judging it.

What I have recognized in ministry is the people who judges a place and right it off do not do anything or extraordinarily little for the Lord, however they are quick to judge instead of praying and asking God to send spirit filled believers to evangelize the city. We must understand that Christ came for everyone. Remember, Jesus came for the sick and we all tend to drift from our creator from time to time.

The Bible clearly teaches,

"For the son of man came to seek and to save the lost."

Luke 19:10

I choose to look for ways in sharing the gospel of Jesus Christ and being in Las Vegas will prove what an excellent time I had in ministering to the needs of people. During the week in Las Vegas God use me in a dynamic way bringing over twenty-five people to Jesus Christ as their personal savior and Lord.

I have decided to document only twelve instances in great depth; however, I will mention the others for you to see how the Lord used me there. Remember, God is no respecter of person, if He use me, He can use you as well. What God desire is a willing heart to do His work and be led by the Spirit of God. With God remarkable things can be manifested through you. Take time to know our heavenly father and He will use you mightily.

Chapter 2

Workers in the Hotel

Chapter 2

Workers in the Hotel

Our travel to Las Vegas was quite enjoyable and relaxing. We arrived in Las Vegas at 430pm on Monday 26 October 2020. We arrived at the Hotel and approached the check in desk, when I noticed that there were two reservation clerks. I looked at one of the clerks and said hello to her and how are you doing today? She responded by saying, "she is doing ok,"

I further prompted her by asking her why ok, she said, "nothing really." When I took upon myself to informed her that I am a Pastor, and I would like to pray with you to accept Jesus Christ as your personal savior and Lord if that is okay with you. She responded by saying, "yes I would love that." I invited her to pray the salvation prayer of which she did and was overly excited to do so. When she said to me "can you pray for my other co-worker who is in the back office?"

I said yes, and she called her co-worker out to meet me and I prayed with her as well and she accepted Jesus Christ as her personal savior and Lord. I gave them a Bible each which I brought with me on the trip. I asked them their names and printed their names and gave them a Bible each, while printing their names, putting the date of their salvation, and writing today is their spiritual birthday. They were so excited, and they thanked me very much, for praying for them and they both said, "that they felt so peaceful and relaxed after praying for them."

The Bible teaches,

"Don't forget to do good and to share what you have because God is pleased with these kinds of sacrifices."

Hebrews 13:6

"In the same way, let your light shine before people, so they can see the good things you do and praise your father who is in heaven."

Matthew 5:16

These two clerks were so happy to know that they had the opportunity to pray the salvation prayer and accepted Jesus Christ as their personal savior and Lord. I said to them God bless you and have a wonderful rest of the day. I left their presence to go to my room and relax for a short while. While about to enter our room, we found out that the key card was not opening the door because the cleaning crew had not finished cleaning the room for us to get into the room.

We called the reservation desk to inform them of the problem and they apologized for the mishap, and they offered us another room and they said they will send the security officer with the keys for us to enter the new room they gave us. We did not have any issues and waited for the security officer to give us the new key card. When the security officer arrived, we greeted each other, and I took the opportunity to minister the gospel of Jesus Christ with her.

She was open for me to pray for her, and while I was praying for her, she was crying, so Gail and I asked her was everything okay, she responded by saying, "NO." We furthered enquired of her, and she said, "her dad practiced another religion, from her mother and she was a bit confused of which is the right religion to follow, however I have a desire to follow Christianity.

It was a breath of fresh air hearing those words coming out of her mouth. I asked her name, and I gave her one of the Bibles I brought with me on the trip. Gail and I saw a burden that was lifted off her shoulder. She thanks us immensely from her heart and said to us, "we are, truly servants of God because she needed clarity concerning deciding to follow Jesus Christ and we came and answer most of the question she needed answered. Thank you, Jesus for using us to bring help to a confused soul. We are always looking for ways to be of aid to people who need services spiritually.

Chapter 3

Souls within the Organization

Chapter 3

Souls within the organization

Well Gail and I finished ministering to the security officer and completed unpacking our luggage. Gail decided to rest a bit; however, I wanted to look around the hotel. As I arrived at the lobby of the hotel, I saw a few new reservation clerks for the night shift. I greeted one of the clerks and introduced myself when one of the clerks said to me, "you are the pastor that prayed for my fellow co-workers earlier in the day."

I responded by saying yes, I am, and I would like to pray for the other reservation clerks as well. One of the clerks said, "yes that will be nice," and I went ahead to pray for her, when suddenly two of her other co-workers were in the back office heard and they came outside, and I had the opportunity to pray for the other three workers.

The Bible teaches,

"I have come into the world as light, so that whoever believes in me may not remain in darkness."

John 12:46

God is so wonderful that I led five reservation clerks to the Lord Jesus Christ and two of them were presented gifts of Bibles because I ran out of Bibles since I only brought five Bibles on the trip. I was so excited because I started off leading two of the reservation clerks to the Lord and the other clerks with their friends to come to Christ.

I saw myself doing well, therefore, the next day I saw some other reservations clerks in the office. I introduced myself and other office staff said, "they heard about me, and it made it easier for me to minister the gospel of Jesus Christ with the other workers.

I had the opportunity to minister and lead the following staff members and guest to the Lord Jesus Christ at the hotel/resort.

- Nine reservation clerks
- The maintenance worker
- The janitor
- In addition, the gospel was shared with a few others.

The word of God went forth with power and clarity, some were believers and others were just not ready to make the commitment to live for the Lord Jesus Christ. I encouraged those that did not accept the Lord Jesus Christ as their personal savior and Lord, that they should not hesitate because you are not promised to be alive the next minute far more to think that you may be alive tomorrow.

I am constantly praying for those who accepted Jesus Christ as their personal savior, that they will live a life committed to the Lord and help bring others to Jesus Christ as well. In addition, I am praying for those who did not accept the Lord that they will realize that only Jesus Christ will make every crocked path in their lives straight.

The Bible teaches,

"Do not boast about tomorrow, for you do not know what a day may bring."

Proverbs 27:1

"Why, you do not even know what will happen tomorrow, what is your life? You are a midst that appears for a little while and then vanishes."

James 4:14

I would like to inform you, my reader, that as the scriptures mentioned above, you do not know what will happen to you the next five minutes of your life. There are instances where people leave to go to work and never make it there safely, some people go to the supermarket and are gunned down by some disturbed individual. When you get the opportunity to pray the salvation prayer to accept Jesus Christ do so at once.

Time is running out, when you get the opportunity embrace it and live a life unto Jesus Christ, he will help you to live a victorious life in Christ Jesus, not a perfect life because there is no such thing as a perfect life on this side of heaven. I am reminded of the scripture found in the Holy Bible,

"So, if the son sets you free, you will be free indeed."

John 8:36

"But thanks be to god, who gives us the victory through our Lord Jesus Christ."

1 Corinthians 15:57

"For it is God who works in you, both to will and to work for his good pleasure."

Philippians 2:13

I met so many interesting people at the resort/hotel. Some of the people were interesting and others were a bit unique in their thought process. For example, I met a young lady who were very dishearten about the Lord, because she was a believer of Christ and had several challenges in her life. Her husband of many years decided to end the marriage, and she was about to be placed on modified work hours. It broke Gail and my heart because she looked disturbed, and we said that we would pray for her on a regular basis, and it lifted her spirit. I reminded her of the scripture found in the Holy Bible,

"But God is faithful, He will not suffer you to be tempted beyond that which you are able to bear, but with the temptation will also make a way to escape, that you may be able to bear it."

1 Corinthians 10:13

On hearing the scripture, it lifted her countenance, and she was able to smile and know that God is willing and able to see her through every demanding situation in her life. We are living a challenging and difficult period, and we can only make it if we put our complete trust in the Lord Jesus Christ.

Another instance I noticed the maintenance worker cleaning and painting the resort and I looked at him and said, good morning and he responded by saying, "good morning." I said to him I came to pray with you to accept Jesus Christ as your personal savior and Lord, would you like me to pray with you, and he responded by saying, "yes I will love to."

I prayed with him and, "he was delighted to accept the Lord Jesus Christ. The next day I saw the janitor doing some minor cleaning and I also greeted him and shared the gospel of Jesus Christ, and he responded by saying, "yes to Jesus Christ as his personal savior and Lord. It was a productive day in ministering the gospel of Jesus Christ with the people of the resort and I was happy to know that I was able to share and minister the gospel with as many people in the resort/hotel.

I completed my work of evangelizing to the workers and guests of the resort. I took my gifting and talents outside the resort by going on the Las Vegas strip to conduct the work the lord has entrusted me to do in the Nevada area on my vacation to celebrate our 25 Wedding Anniversary. Thank you, Jesus.

Chapter 4

The Restaurant worker

Chapter 4

The Restaurant worker

Gail and I got up early the next morning and decided to take a nice long walk around the resort we were staying in. We planned the day's activity incredibly early because we were trying to beat the hot weather that Las Vegas is noted for. We took a nice long walk on the strip and the back roads just to see the place. We visited most of the hotels and casinos, seeing people's behaviors and the way people were going about their lives.

We walked about three to four miles on the strip and some of the things we noticed were not pleasant to the eyes, in terms of the way some of these young people dressed and the way they cared about themselves. However, I was not quick to judge them because I know that people need the Lord. I was reminded of the scriptures found in the Bible,

"For all have sinned and fall short of the glory of God."

Romans 3:23

"The law was brought in so that the trespass might increase. But where sin increased, grace increased even more."

Romans 5:20

We were exhausted and hungry after walking for about four to five miles and were looking for a restaurant that served seafood. We entered a food plaza and noticed a seafood eatery. I approached the greeter at the restaurant about the food they served. He offered me the menu and said, "are you looking for good food" I responded by saying yes, and I found the question he asked me was a bit strange. I turned to him and said, you offer physical food, however, I come to offered you spiritual food in the personality of Jesus Christ as your personal savior and Lord.

I said to him would you like me to pray for you to accept Jesus Christ as your personal savior and Lord now? He responded by saying, "yes I would like to accept him." I prayed with him the salvation prayer and he accepted Jesus Christ as his savior and Lord.

He said, "thank you sir, I felt something while we were praying." I mentioned it was the power of God upon you, "he said wow and we both simile and I walked away, and he was called by one of his co-workers to deal with a customer. The Bible is full of his word concerning people embracing the Lord Jesus Christ.

"Jesus answered, "it I written: Man shall not live by bread alone, but on every word that comes from the mouth of God."

Matthew 4:4

I was elated in the way the Lord use me to minister to the young man who offered physical food to me, and the Lord uses it by his holy spirit to allow me to share with him the importance of spiritual food that was needed for him. Thank you, Lord for using me to bring this young man to you. He was so happy and the way he looked at me and he was so sincere in his thoughts towards me. As the name of the book illustrates LOOK AT MY GOD.

"Gracious words are a honeycomb, sweet to the soul and healing to the bones."

Proverbs 16:24

I pray God grant this young man favor in his life and may God continue to use him to bring other people to the Lord and be the light in a dark place wherever he goes because of his demeanor after being prayed for, he looks like a person God can use in the kingdom of God.

Chapter 5

Office workers

Chapter 5

Office workers

An associate invited Gail and I to see a presentation and we took the opportunity and while we were in the meeting there were several office staff at the company. I ministered to a young lady from the country of Cuba about the Lord Jesus Christ, and she was a little reluctant at the beginning and I press on further about the importance of living for Jesus Christ after which I noticed that she was becoming more receptive to the gospel.

I was very patient with her until and I realized that she was coming around to the leading of the Holy Spirit, when I said to myself that she is ready and I asked her, if she would like me to pray with her to receive Jesus Christ as her personal savior and Lord. She responded by saying, "yes." I prayed with her the salvation prayer, and she accepted Jesus Christ as her personal savior and Lord in the office. After she prayed the salvation prayer, she informs me that, "she felt chills in her body and wanted to know what that was." I shared with her that it was the Holy Spirit of God ministering to her, of which she was excited.

On conclusion of praying for her I presented her with a Bible and asked her to give me her mobile number so that we can further correspond with each other. I communicated with her the next day via text message, and she shared with me when she got home, she informed her family members what had happened in the office the previous day. Sharing the gospel of Jesus Christ takes patience and compassion to fulfill the call of God upon your life.

The Bible teaches,

"Therefore, as God's chosen people, holy and dearly loved, clothe yourselves with compassion, kindness, humility, gentleness, and patience.

Colossians 3:12

The next day Gail and I went to pay a courtesy visit at the office with the lady I led to Jesus Christ the previous day, when a young lady from the country of Morocco approached me and said to me, "I saw you yesterday at the office and I wanted to speak to you about an important matter." I said sure and we spoke briefly.

I answered the question she needed answered to and I took the opportunity and asked her if she would like me to pray for her to accept Jesus Christ as her personal savior and Lord. She responded by saying, "yes, I will like that. I prayed the salvation prayer with her, and she accepted Jesus Christ as her personal savior and Lord. She thanked me very much because she needed that. Thank you, Lord, for using me to bring salvation to two people in an office. The Bible teaches,

"Preach the word; be prepared in season and out of season; correct, rebuke, and encourage with great patience and careful instruction. For the time will come when men will not put up with sound doctrine."

2 Timothy 4:2

Chapter 6

Aquatic Workers

Chapter 6

Aquatic workers

We were given free passes for Gail and me to attend the aquarium. We got up early that morning and traveled to the aquarium to see some unique, different, beautiful, and attractive displays of a variety of species of aquatic mammals and animals. We arrived early and waited for about thirty minutes for us to enter the aquarium. However, it gave me the opportunity to show my friendly behavior and my gifting in evangelism.

I walked around the facility looking for anyone I can minister the gospel of Jesus Christ to, when I saw a young man approaching my direction, we both exchanged some pleasantries. I said to him how are you doing today he said, "I am doing fine and how are you doing as well. He responded by telling me am doing very well. He said, "great." I said I would like to pray with you because I am a Pastor, and I love to pray for people. He responded by saying that "will be great because I am going through a lot right now." We both bowed our heads and prayed together, and he said to me, "thank you very much he needed that today."

I asked him would you like me to pray for you to accept Jesus Christ as your personal savior and Lord? He looked at me and smile and said, "I am a Christian." I said great and I gave him some Bible scriptures to read to help strengthen him during this challenging time in his life, The Scripture, I gave him was 1 Peter 5:7

"Casting all your cares upon Jesus, for he cares for you."

1 Peter 5:7

We parted ways and I said to him, may God bless you and cause his light to shine upon you and give you success.

So, there was time for us to redeem our tickets and pursue the wonderful adventure of looking at the beautiful animals. We approached the ticket clerk and I in my usual way greeter her and because it was only Gail and myself in line, I had the wonderful opportunity to share the gospel of Jesus Christ with the admission clerk. I asked her if you would like to accept Jesus Christ as your personal savior and Lord?

She responded by saying, "yes." I after prayed with her the salvation prayer, and she accepted Jesus as her Lord and savior. The Bible teaches,

"Jesus said to them, "Go into all the world and preach the gospel to all creation."

Mark 16:15

As mentioned in my earlier illustration in this book. Go is an action word, and we must be committed to doing God's word.

We followed the direction of the clerk, and we went ahead to look at the animals. When I looked and saw a couple approaching us and we just said hello to them and exited. It was interesting to see some animals that I have not seen either for a long time or have never seen in my life apart from seeing them on television. I saw some piranhas, which are freshwater fish that inhabit South American lakes and rivers. In addition, we saw a Komodo dragon, which is the largest extant species of lizard growing up to ten feet long and it is a native of the Indonesians islands.

Viewing those mammals was a treat for us and having to see and leading two staff members to Jesus Christ was an added treat for us. The two staff members were excited to accept Jesus Christ as their personal savior and Lord and they thank me for sharing the gospel of Jesus Christ quickly and yet it came with clarity. I am forever grateful to the Lord Jesus Christ for giving me a unique way of sharing the gospel and at the same time it is done quickly and yet powerfully done.

The Bible teaches,

"Don't you know that when you offer yourself to someone as obedient salves, you are salves of the one you obey -whether you are slaves to sin, which leads to death, or to obedience, which leads to righteousness?"

Romans 6:16

Chapter 7

Asian Brother

Chapter 7

Asian Brother

Gail and I when looking at a store to replenish some items we had finished. We arrived at the store and I being a gregarious person, I am always looking for ways to meet and greet people, with the intention of steering them to the Lord, Jesus Christ. The Bible teaches,

"A man who has friends must himself be friendly."

Proverbs 18:24a

We approached the store, and I said hello to the first couple of people I met, and they responded in a cordial manner. An important concept to grasp here is, if you want to minister to the needs of people, you must conduct yourself in a friendly manner. When you are friendly to people you break the ice of animosity and give people an opportunity to interact with you.

It is difficult to minister to people without being friendly and greeting them. This is one of my easier ways to minister to people, greet them and be friendly to them, after which I approach them with the gospel of Jesus Christ, so it become easier for them to be receptive to the gospel and most importantly, depend on the Holy Spirit for wisdom, guidance and compassion.

So, I approached a young lady in the store, and she was pleasant to me, and I asked her if she would like me to pray for her? She responded, by saying, "No, I am an atheist." I asked her why that decision to become an atheist? She said, I do not believe that God exist because of the things that are going on in the world, for example the evil." I said to her, you cannot blame God for man's evil desires and disobedience to his commands. She further irritated, "she has to go back to work."

Later in the shopping journey I met a young man, and we spoke briefly, and I asked if he would like me to pray for him to accept Jesus Christ his personal savior and Lord today? He responded by saying, "yes."

This young man of Asian descent was so receptive and willing to take time from his busy schedule to pray with me at the entrance of the store because that was important to him, and he was going through some difficult in his life or today was just the acceptable time for his salvation.

The Bible teaches,

"For he says, "in the time of my favor I heard you, and in the day of salvation I helped you." T tell you, now is the time of God's favor, now is the day of Salvation."

2 Corinthians 6:2

Today was the day of Salvation for my Asian brother. God set him up to meet me. A person travelling from California to Las Vegas to meet him. Thank you, Lord, and for everyone who accepted Jesus Christ throughout this book their lives will never be the same again and they will live in victory.

Chapter 8

International Salvation

Chapter 8

International Salvation

Well after ministering to my Asian brother and salvation came to his home. Gail and I set out to enjoy the local Eiffel tower at one of the Las Vegas casinos. I decided to go on to see what the thrill was about. We got our tickets, and I went ahead to follow my wife on the Eiffel experience. We arrived at the top of the tower and when I looked down my head started to hurt me, of which I did not know what was causing it, I stayed for a little while longer and my head continued hurting me. I did not know what the cause was, either it was the speed at which they went to the top level or the heat of the day.

Therefore, I mentioned to Gail the problem I was having, and I decided to come down and wait for her downstairs in the casino area of the hotel. When at once my head stopped hurting me, which was a sign of relief. When existing the elevator, I saw one of the workers and she asked me, "what was wrong that I came off so quicky."

So, I took the time to explain to her the problem I was having and the opportunity to share the gospel of Jesus Christ with her. She was so receptive to the gospel, and I was aware in my spirit that she was ready to accept the Lord. She said, at once, "I will love to pray to accept the Lord Jesus Christ." I was elated to know the process was so quick and she was happy to accept the Lord. As mentioned above the day of her salvation was now.

One of her co-workers saw me and said to her that, "I cannot be on the platform I will have to go downstairs and exit the platform area." I said that is okay because I told Gail previously, I will wait for her in the lobby. I went ahead to go downstairs and look around the casino area and I glazed upon a young man of Asian descent for the Philippines who just arrive to the USA about four months ago. We spoke for a few minutes, and I minister the gospel of Jesus Christ with him. I further asked him if he would like to accept Jesus Christ as his personal savior and Lord and he said, "yes I will love to pray with you, and you are a nice and respectable man."

He prayed the salvation prayer, and he was happy to accept Jesus Christ as his personal savior and lord. I was happy to be a part of his salvation experience, all to the glory of God. The next day we went to experience the glandular boat ride and as always, my evangelist mindset overtake me, and I was led to share the gospel of Jesus Christ with one of the Italian girl who was serenading us on the ride and a Filipino young man who was our tour guide on the ride. They both accept Jesus Christ as their personal savior and Lord.

The Bible teaches,

"But *you, keep your head in all situations, endure hardship, do the work of an evangelist, discharge all the duties of your ministry.*"

2 Timothy 4:5

"For Christ did not send me to baptize, but to preach the gospel – not with wisdom and eloquence, lest the cross of Christ be emptied of the power.

1 Corinthians 1:17

Chapter 9

Girls on the Strip

Chapter 9

Girls on the strip

Gail and I enjoy walking and sightseeing on the strip as mentioned in my earlier chapter we walk for about four to five miles. Our intention daily is to walk about ten thousand steps a day. Our steps are tracked and recorded on our cell phones. We looked at our phone and we were near our goal of ten thousand steps a day, so we went ahead to walk back to our hotel.

As were walking back to the hotel we noticed three African American women walking towards our direction and I was moved with compassion to approached them. I stop them and say to then I would like to pray with the three of you to accept Jesus Christ as their personal savior and Lord of which they responded by saying, "yes we will love to." They stopped in the middle of the sideway and they all prayed the salvation prayer to accept the Lord.

I was happy to know they stopped and allow me to pray for them to accept the Lord. They said, "thank you for praying for us." When I looked back, I saw they were looking at me and smiling and I perceived that they were happy to accept the Lord, and I was happy that I can be used as a vessel to bring salvation to these ladies.

The Bible teaches,

"The Lord is gracious and righteous; our God is full of compassion."

Psalm 116:5

"Then Jesus said to his disciples, "the harvest is plentiful, but the workers are few." Ask the Lord of the harvest, therefore, to send out workers into his harvest field."

Matthew 9:37-38

On my trip to Las Vegas for one week God use me to lead people from the following countries: =

- United States of America
- Mexico
- Cuba
- Italy
- Philippines
- Morocco

With a total of twenty-six coming to Jesus Christ as their personal savior and Lord, all to the glory of God. It was a successful trip because we celebrated and enjoyed our twenty-five years of wedding anniversary, and many souls came to the Lord and many more was ministered too. Thank you, Jesus, for using me in a dynamic way on the trip.

I know by the grace of God that I am one of the workers willing to go into the harvest and bring people to the Lord Jesus Christ as their savior and Lord. We need to be people willing to do the work of the Lord because so many people are hurting and in desperate need of a savior who is willing and capable of healing and setting them free.

Chapter 10

Adventurous ministry

Chapter 10

Adventurous Ministry

Ministry requires a level of boldness, commitment, and compassion to conduct the work out the work of the Lord.

The Bible teaches,

"The wicked flee through no one pursues, but the righteous are as bold as a lion."

Proverbs 28:1

During our time in Las Vegas for a week God allowed me the distinct opportunity to minister to people of different ethnic and cultural backgrounds. I love meeting the needs of people and travelling to Las Vegas was no difference.

I recalled one instance looking at two young ladies that was dressed needing a lot to be wanted of when I approached them and one of the ladies was receptive to hearing the gospel and her friend insisted that she come on and not waste their time. Therefore, the leader of the two ladies insists telling her friend, "Come on, come on, we do not need to hear that at this moment, we have things to do." I was a bit disappointed because.

I felt in my spirit that the girl wanted to hear more about the redeeming quality of Jesus Christ and what he can do in her life. However, I was not willing to pursue her further to hear the word of God, because the word of God must have it free course to minister to the needs of people. We are commanded to share the gospel and allow the Holy Spirit to convict them of their short coming. I trust God will raise someone to minister the gospel with these two young ladies and make Jesus Christ their personal savior and Lord. May God grant them the success, victory and help them to lead others to the Lord.

Remember, God is no respecter of person, and he is willing that none perish but all come into the saving knowledge of Jesus Christ and live a life that is in union with God.

Chapter 11

Final analysis

Chapter 11

Final Analysis

In my final analysis, I want to inform all my reader, that it is important to pray and seek the Lord for direction on how we go about bringing people into a relationship with our Lord and savior Jesus Christ. God did not call us to be judges and executioner, but to minister the Love of God with everyone we meet.

I am forever grateful to my heavenly father for giving me the opportunity to bring so many people to Jesus Christ as their personal savior and Lord. I never take my calling lightly; however, I try my best to spend time in the presence of the Lord daily to make my calling an election sure and gifting a surety.

When I get to Heaven, I want to hear my Lord and savior Jesus Christ say well done good and faithful servant, enter the joy of the Lord. What will be disheartening to some is to hear the Lord say, to them depart from me you worker of iniquity.

I believe, why the Lord will say that to some people is because they did the work of the Lord for their self-glorification and not to bring honor to God. We, as ministers, must be careful what we do, and why we do what we do.

It is important to ask the Lord to make me and mold me into the image of our savior. I see so many ministers and preachers conducing themselves as if the are God on the earth. They seek the worship of men, and they act like if they are God incarnate on the earth. What a terrible thing it is to fall into the hands of the living God. If I recalled in scripture, Satan fell because he wanted to be like the most high God. We can desire to be like God, but not to be God. There is a major difference, unfortunately, so many do not understand the difference.

I will explain the concept mentioned above. To be like God, is to adopt the personalities and traits of God. The ability to go about doing good and to be moved and be led with compassion. On the other hand, to be God means that you assume to be the creator and supreme being of heaven. God created you; you cannot be the creator and the created being all at the same time.

We need to check ourselves to see if we are in right standing with God daily, because it is extremely easy to lose track and become conceited. Remember, God resist the proud but give grace to the humble. Humble yourself under the mighty hand of God, so that He can use you to bring change and deliverance to a lost and dying world. Stay loving Jesus Christ.

I want to challenge everyone to pursue God at all costs. He will never leave you, nor will he forsake you.

The Bible teaches,

"Come near to God and he will come near to you Wash your hands, you sinners, and purify your hearts, you double minded."

James 4:8

The greatest thing you can do for the kingdom of God, is to share the gospel with everyone you meet and help make disciples of men. God is calling you today, to be on His father's business an to focus on doing His work and complete it to the end.

Chapter 12

Have Compassion

Chapter 12

Have Compassion

People always asked me this all-important question. How do you lead so many people to Jesus Christ as their personal savior and Lord? Do you have a formular for bringing people to Jesus Christ as often as you do? I always reply to them by saying, you must be moved and led by the Holy Spirit and have a heart full of compassion. People need Jesus Christ as their personal savior and Lord. Without having a relationship with Jesus Christ is very detrimental, because when you died without having Jesus Christ as your savior, you will not make it into heaven.

The Bible teaches,

Jesus replied, "Very truly I tell you, no one can see the kingdom of God unless they are born again."

John 3:3

"For the wages of sin is death, but the gift of God is eternal life in Christ Jesus our Lord."

Romans 6:23

"Whoever believes in the son has eternal life, but whoever rejects the son will not see life, for God's wrath remains on them."

John 3:36

Based on the scriptures mentioned above you see why it is important to have a relationship with our Lord and savior Jesus Christ. He is our soon and coming king. He is willing that none perish but all come into a saving knowledge of the truth that Jesus Christ is Lord of all. Trust him at his word, he will never leave you, neither will he forsake you. God loves you with an everlasting love. Give him a chance and see what great things you can accomplish in your life.

Conclusion

We are living in challenging times, and we need all the help we can get from our heavenly father. Without the aid of our heavenly father life will be difficult for us. So many people believe that they can live this life apart from God, they are deceiving themselves and I pray God help them maneuver and come out victorious.

There is no life apart from God's help, I am a living testimony of God's grace upon my life. I could have been dead over ten times, order the book on my life, entitled "I AM ALIVE," to get a clearer understanding of living a transform life. God is willing and able to set you through every demanding situation in your life, the important concept to grasp is you must put your whole trust in God.

On my daily evangelistic work, I come across all types and mindset of people and it have me thinking what is going on with people in the world today. Due to all this confusion, I have decided to intensify my prayer life towards the young people that they will find their way in Jesus' name.

What is very disturbing to me is that so many young people when I approach them to minister the gospel of Jesus Christ and they inform me that they are agnostic, or atheist and I find it difficult to understand the reason for their decision. I will list a few reasons for some of their decision to walk away from God.

- God does not exist.
- Too much evil in the world
- They believe in science.
- The big bang theory
- You do not need a God, because you are a god.
- There is no heaven for there to be a God.
- People are being misled into thinking that there is a God.
- People are being brainwashed.
- They have many problems in attending church.
- Church goers are hypocrites.

At the time of authoring this book I did not have a church. However, so many people are encouraging me to open a church and start preaching every week in a building. I have a ministry called Divine Ministries and my wife conducts several ministry outreaches throughout the year ministering to the needs of families. We conduct men's seminars and women's seminars. We used to conduct Bible studies for high school students and marriage seminars but due to the Covid19 pandemic we had to scaled back on these programs. We are both certified marriage mentors and marriage facilitators supplying help to younger marriage couples to have better marriages thereby leaving a godly example for other marriages to follow.

I want to encourage all those who want to be more effective and start leading people to Jesus Christ ask God's Holy Spirit to empower you and give you the boldness and courage to share the gospel of Jesus Christ.

Remember, God desire.

"All people save and come to a knowledge of the truth."

1 Timothy 2:4

"Jesus replied, "verily, verily I tell you, no one can see the kingdom of God unless they are born again."

John 3:3

Therefore, if Jesus want all men, women and children be saved. I would like to see everyone save as well. He encourages you to win the lost for Christ too, do not be afraid God will help you through. Stay committed to the call of God upon your life. As mentioned, above, I do not have a church, but I disciple some of the people I led to Jesus Christ. I visit some of them regularly in person, others via text messages and via other platforms on social media and wherever means of connecting with them.

Qualifications to be born-Again.

Ephesians 2:8-9

For by grace, you have been saved through faith, and not through anything that you have done. It is a gift from God and did not come about through working for it. In case anyone wants to boast.

1. Admit you are a sinner, having broken and transgressed against God's laws, and need a savior. Romans 6:23

2. Believe in Jesus Christa the son of God who died to pay for our sins? John 3:3 and John 3:16

3. Repent for your sins. Romans 10:9 and 1 John 1:9

4. Accept Jesus Christ as your personal savior and Lord. John 3:3

5. Please direct attention to the next section and pray for the salvation prayer. The Lord is waiting for you my reader, to come to Him because of his impressive love for you. His arms are wide open to accept you into the body of Christ. He paid the ultimate price for your sins.

He is waiting for your response to Him, so you may have a life more abundantly. Life is too precious to waste, and he will give you a life to your fullest potential in Him.

To the unbeliever and the person who wants to give, or re-dedicate their life to Christ, please pray the salvation prayer on the following page.

If you made a commitment to live for Jesus Christ for the rest of your life, please email me and let me know of your new birth experience. See my contact page for more information on being part of the family of God, which is the greatest family you could ever be part of. Stay blessed forever my siblings in Christ.

The Salvation Prayer

Dear Jesus Christ,

I come to you just as I am a sinner, and I confess all my past and present sins before you. Help me to live a truly Christian life following your word. From now on, dear God. I will live only for you, by your grace and mercy. Thank you for saving me, in Jesus' name.

If you have prayed this prayer and believe in Christ in your heart. The Bible states that you are now Born-Again.

"I tell you the truth; no one can see the kingdom of God unless he is born-again."

John 3:3

Celebrate your new birth by finding a home church where the undefiled and pure word of God is taught. The Lord will equip, strengthen, and encourage you to live a life that is above reproach.

I would like to know that you are being taught well, advancing the things of God, making valuable contributions to the kingdom, and most importantly, that you are putting to flight demons who are oppressing people.

The Lord will work through you, if you allow Him to do so in the process, therefore do not hesitate to send me an email and let me know how you are doing. See my contact page.

We hope that you enjoyed the valuable time of teaching with Pastor Caprietta.

If you would like to contact Pastor Caprietta for added copies of this book or other books, schedule a speaking engagement or check his events please contact:

Pastors Paul M and Gail P. Caprietta

Co-laborers

www.divineministriesinc.org

office: 562-806-0969

Email: <u>pastorcaprietta@hotmail.com</u>

Visit amamzon.com by searching for Paul Caprietta and refer all friends and family members to these life-changing and inspirational books.

I would like to encourage my reader to get the following books by the same author, so that your knowledge and understanding of winning the lost for Jesus Christ will be strengthen. Please take time to look at some of my books on the following pages. You will find these books to be immensely helpful, life-changing, and thought-provoking. Your life will never be the same after reading these formidable books.

Thank you for taking time out of your busy schedule to be inspired as you read these books. Once again, thank you in advance for your support. Remember, whatever you do for God will last forever and God will bless you richly.

Books of the same series for your reading pleasure

Look at My God! 2
Victories in Evangelism
Pastor Paul Caprietta

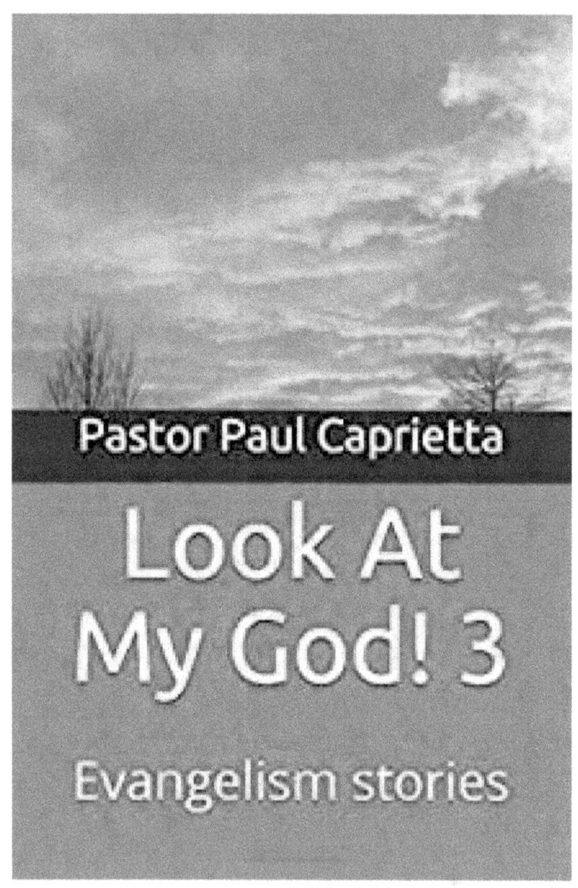
Pastor Paul Caprietta
Look At
My God! 3
Evangelism stories

Look
At My
God 4
Stories in Winning souls
Paul Caprietta

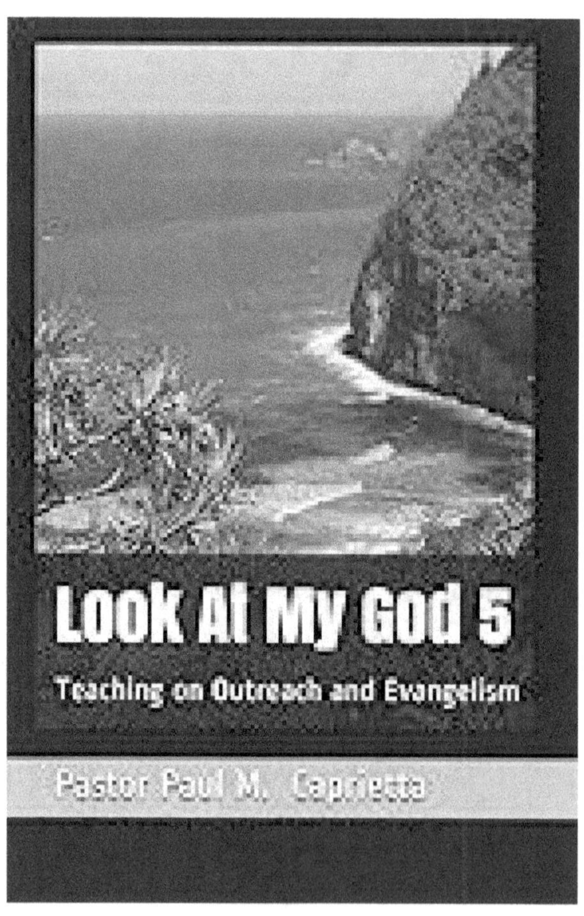
Look At My God 5
Teaching on Outreach and Evangelism
Pastor Paul M. Caprietta

Put your trust in God.

He will never let you down.

Commit your ways.

to the Jesus Christ

and he will give you.

the desires of your heart

Jesus Christ is calling you.

into a relationship with him now.

Cast all your Cares upon Jesus because he cares for you.

Serve the Lord

While you are young

I have decided.

To follow

Jesus Christ

Give Jesus Christ Your everything

Note taking.

Note Taking

Note Taking

Note Taking

www.ingramcontent.com/pod-product-compliance
Lightning Source LLC
Chambersburg PA
CBHW071042250726
48653CB00005B/1949